D0996702

INSPIRATION
FOR
every
day

LIZZIE CORNWALL

summersdale

INSPIRATION FOR EVERY DAY

Summersdale Publishers Ltd
46 West Street
Chichester
West Sussex
PO19 1RP
UK

www.summersdale.com

Printed and bound in China

ISBN: 978-1-78685-232-8

Substantial discounts on bulk quantities of Summersdale books are available to corporations, professional associations and other organisations. For details contact general enquiries: telephone: +44 (0) 1243 771107 or email: enquiries@summersdale.com.

To...........................

From........................

Join a yoga or t'ai chi class – both
will help you be physically stronger,
mentally calmer and better prepared
to face your personal challenges.

Get yourself a penfriend or online friend in another country, so you can swap notes on your experiences of living in your respective cultures. Write whenever you can.

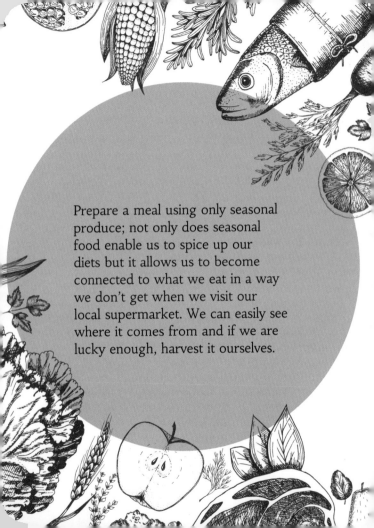

Prepare a meal using only seasonal produce; not only does seasonal food enable us to spice up our diets but it allows us to become connected to what we eat in a way we don't get when we visit our local supermarket. We can easily see where it comes from and if we are lucky enough, harvest it ourselves.

Seasonal food also comes with new opportunities and experiences, consider taking a walk in a local forest to gather your own sweet chestnuts to roast, or even learn how to prepare venison and guinea fowl from a local butcher.

You may discover something new to enjoy, such as a taste of a food you never thought you would like, perhaps the walk to a local produce provider, or even the challenge of a new recipe.

Take a different route to
work and take special notice
of your new surroundings.

Catch
the trade winds
in your sails.
Explore. Dream. Discover.

H. Jackson Brown Jr

Consider one of your daily routines – could it be improved? If so, how? Do you find yourself in a rush in the mornings? Do you find yourself feeling overly tired in the evenings, but you still have so much to do before bed?

Often we spend time doing things that don't actually benefit us. For example, perhaps you're not a morning person, but you need to be up bright and early for work.

Think about all the things you do in your morning routine – does everything need to be done in the morning? You could, for instance, organise your bag, plan the next day's outfit, or prepare a breakfast that can be stored overnight. Doing so means that when your alarm goes off in the morning you can take a few extra minutes to wake up naturally, focusing on the dream you just had or what you're going to achieve in the day ahead, instead of feeling like you need to jump up and into the shower immediately.

Go into your garden or local park, pick a tree and draw it in as much detail as possible. Make a date to visit the tree in spring, summer, autumn and winter and record how it's changed by drawing it again.

Imagination will take you everywhere.

Albert Einstein

Find a local cooking class that uses food you have not cooked with before; look at classes featuring a cuisine you're unfamiliar with to get yourself started. You might find your new favourite meal. Similarly, if you see a recipe on a cooking show or in the newspaper that gets your mouth watering, get down to the supermarket, find the ingredients and start cooking!

Try your hand at working with papier mâché. A favourite material of school projects, it's easy to make at home and a great start for making little sculptures or props for costumes.

Infinite

Creative

energy flows

through you

MY MISSION IN LIFE IS NOT
MERELY TO SURVIVE, BUT
TO THRIVE; AND TO DO
SO WITH SOME PASSION,
SOME COMPASSION, SOME
HUMOUR, AND SOME STYLE.

Maya Angelou

THE MAN WHO
REMOVES A
MOUNTAIN BEGINS
BY CARRYING AWAY
SMALL STONES.

Chinese proverb

Visit your local church, temple, mosque or synagogue. Even if you are not religious, or belong to a different faith, take the time to appreciate the architecture and the atmosphere of a place of worship.

LOVING
YOURSELF
IS ITS
OWN ART.

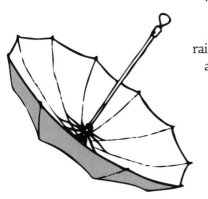

When it rains, walk
as if it is a sunny
day. Embrace the
raindrops and become
at one with nature
– it's liberating.

Leave your TV, laptop and mobile phone turned off all afternoon. Spend your time absorbing the sights, smells and sounds of your neighbourhood.

Nothing
really
matters
except
what
you
do
now
in this
instant
of time.

Eileen Caddy

Close your eyes and imagine yourself
waking up in five years' time. What does
your room look like? Are you alone
or with someone? What do you wear?
Use these images to spur you on to
attain your goals. Murals take time and
many small brushstrokes to paint, so it
is important to make sure we can also
visualise the steps to getting there.

How about in a year? What do you
see? Have you taken a step towards
those goals? Think about your room
for example, is it the same one you're
in now, or is it in a different home?
It can be overwhelming to only aim for the
end goal. Focus on what you can achieve
now, as it helps paint that big picture, but
also allows you to appreciate what you
have now and what you can change.

Reshuffle the rooms in your house. You might find that you have not yet found the perfect 'Feng Shui' and that moving a bed or rearranging your cupboards helps create a freer, more inspiring environment.

Read your favourite poem aloud. You absorb things in a different way when you speak or listen.

Create a quirky sculpture out of spare
bits and pieces you have lying around –
make it as elaborate as possible. Then take
this sculpture apart and make something
completely different. Open your imagination!

Recognise that **every day** we are the result of **every past decision** we have made,

and **tomorrow** we are going to be the direct result of the decisions we are making **today**. Begin the process to become the **best you can be**.

Embrace your passions. Whatever it is you feel really strongly about, or whatever your talent – share it with others today. Spread your knowledge and enthusiasm. You could do this in a big way, perhaps sharing a poem you've written on social media or in a smaller way by simply showing your writing to a friend in casual conversation. Remember that when you embrace your passions others can see it too. Having an enjoyment and passion for things is infectious, not only will you find social interactions easier when speaking about an interest, but you'll also get reassurance from others that it's alright to love something that your peers may not. Learning to accept yourself for who you are is important, and surrounding yourself with people who share and encourage your passions is a valuable asset.

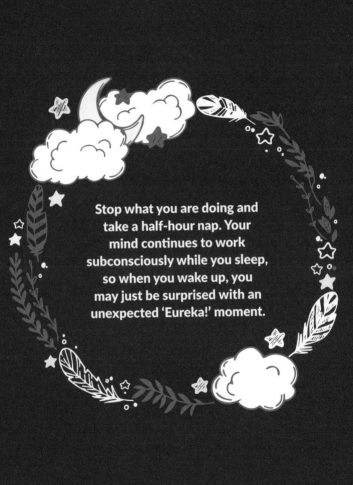

Stop what you are doing and take a half-hour nap. Your mind continues to work subconsciously while you sleep, so when you wake up, you may just be surprised with an unexpected 'Eureka!' moment.

BE NOT SIMPLY GOOD, BE GOOD FOR SOMETHING.

Henry David Thoreau

pleasure

DISAPPOINTS:

POSSIBILITY

never.

Søren Kierkegaard

Make contact with an
old friend – it might
ignite memories that
you had forgotten.

Be a mentor to someone
who would like to learn a
skill that you might have.

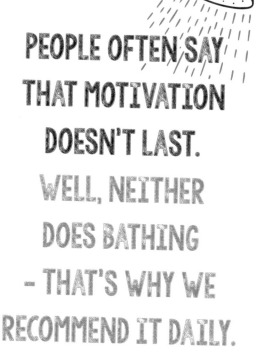

PEOPLE OFTEN SAY
THAT MOTIVATION
DOESN'T LAST.
WELL, NEITHER
DOES BATHING
- THAT'S WHY WE
RECOMMEND IT DAILY.

Zig Ziglar

Volunteer a few hours of your time to a charity shop, hospice or homeless shelter, and strike up friendly conversations with all the people you meet.

Go outside and smell the fresh air. Take deep breaths and really notice everything you can about its smell. Embrace it.

**Stop and
listen to your
favourite music
without any
distractions.**

Write out, by hand, your favourite passage from a great book, or something you've read today that strikes you as powerful. Using a pen and paper will help you connect with the message.

Think about something you take for granted every day – consider how you might do things differently without it.

LIFE BEGINS AT THE END OF YOUR COMFORT ZONE.

Neale Donald Walsch

Set goals to complete
over the coming week:

complete one
sketch per day,

write 1,000 words per day,

cook with one new
ingredient per day –

whatever takes your fancy.

FIND OUT WHAT YOU'RE AFRAID OF AND GO LIVE THERE.

Chuck Palahniuk

GENIUS IS ONE PER CENT INSPIRATION, NINETY-NINE PER CENT PERSPIRATION.

Thomas Edison

Pick out an object that you find cheerful and draw it using wax crayons or coloured pencils with simple, spontaneous lines. Staring at a screen all day can be taxing, an excellent way of taking a break and beating boredom is to doodle. Even if you're not the best at drawing, think of how you could change the object you've chosen – it's simple enough to do a quick scribble. Your favourite mug could become a surreal object, with wings and a tail, or perhaps it's now floating in the middle of a sea under a stormy sky. Share your doodle with someone; you may make them laugh, or even exclaim in delight at how good your 'awful' drawing is.

Embrace the rain
and your inner child:
splash paint onto thick
watercolour paper,
then hold it outside
briefly for the elements
to work their magic.
Use the colourful paper
as the background
for an art project.

Plant basil, tomato or salad-leaf seeds in pots to keep on your windowsill.

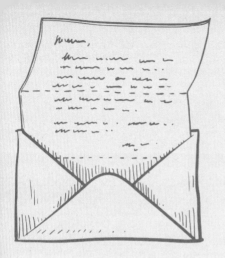

Write a letter to
someone without
using the words
'I', 'me' or 'my'.

With time
and distance
comes
perspective.

Energise yourself with a brisk swim
– outdoors, if possible.

The difference between ordinary and extraordinary is that little extra.

Jimmy Johnson

Branch

BED

DINNER

Drop

B

C

CAR

Cloud

E

Egg

Zebra

ZIGZAG

EYE

Insect

Start a nature diary and record all of the plants and animals you come across while out walking (if you don't know the names, take photos and look them up afterwards).

N

Nest

NOSE

OCEAN

Oak

Tree

RICE

R

Rain
UP!

PENCIL

P

Planet

T

TEA

UMBRELLA

**Make a journey in a way you're
not used to – take the bus to
work, cycle to the pub, take
a taxi to a friend's house.**

Sign up now to take part in a charity run, walk or skydive later in the year, and start preparing for it.

A mind is like a parachute. It doesn't work if it is not open.

Frank Zappa

A spring clean is
always a good idea
– a clear space
is fertile ground
for new ideas.

Dance! Dance like you're Gene Kelly in the rain or Fred Astaire in his top hat. For no real reason, wherever you are.

Write a letter to someone
you've always admired but
have never been in contact
with. You never know,
it could blossom into a
wonderful friendship!

Inspiration comes from saying YES

Take advantage of the asparagus
season (it's short!). Buy in bulk and
make asparagus soup, asparagus
and caramelised onion tarts, grilled
asparagus with goat's cheese...

Spend all day actively listening. If you ask somebody how they are, let them say more than 'fine'. It can be surprising just how much you miss in conversation. Take time to focus on what someone is saying to you – could you help them? Or do they just need that friendly, caring, listening ear? It may end up being both but by taking the time to focus on someone else you show that they are important to you.

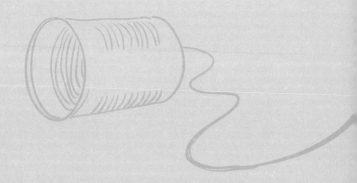

In return, they will most likely be there to listen when you are in the middle of a bad day or want a bit of advice for a problem you may be suffering. Showing you care has endless benefits, some of which will become obvious as your relationships with those you have listened to strengthen, other benefits may be subtle.

Practise the 'Memory Palace' technique (the art of remembering things through mental images) to improve your recall.

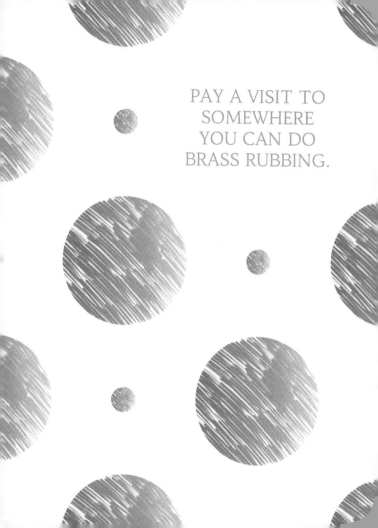

PAY A VISIT TO
SOMEWHERE
YOU CAN DO
BRASS RUBBING.

THE GREATEST MISTAKE YOU CAN MAKE IN LIFE IS TO BE CONTINUALLY FEARING YOU WILL MAKE ONE.

Elbert Hubbard

Arrange a debate night with some close friends. Bring out the tea and biscuits and discuss a current controversial topic. Do some research first and keep it civil – but make it interesting!

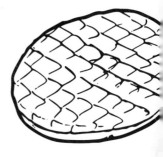

Educate yourself on a religion,
country or culture you know little about.

All life is an
experiment. The
more experiments you
make, the better.

Ralph Waldo Emerson

Go to a poetry reading or open-mic night. Even better: volunteer to read a poem or perform one of your own songs. One of the biggest hurdles in being creative is the fear of being judged for a piece of work you have created. Exploring what other people are willingly putting out there can help build confidence and re-spark the creative juices. Surround yourself with other creative people in the same passion as you, and listen to what they are offering, you could even offer your own feedback to the artist. If you can read or sing something of your own it gives a valuable opportunity to listen to critiques. Those who don't like your work for whatever reason are just as important as those who praise it. It is difficult to grow and develop as an artist without discovering what people like and don't like about your work.

I have found that if you love life, life will love you back.

Arthur Rubinstein

A journey
of a thousand
miles begins with
a single step.

Lao Tzu

The WORLD iS a BOOK aND those WHO DO NOT travel READ ONLY a PaGe.

St Augustine

Keep a notebook and pen next to your
bed and record your dreams as soon as
you wake up. Get a dream dictionary to
interpret their meanings. If you wake up
but you can't remember exactly what
you were dreaming of, you can always
draw how you feel at that moment,
perhaps a smiley face, or a confused one.
A dream diary can simply offer you a bit
of entertainment to read back through,
like a diary from our teenage years.

Dreams can offer you your best ideas if you can save them in time, as they are an endless font of creativity, giving us interesting insights into everyday life you would never have considered whilst awake. If you choose to get a dream dictionary, then the meanings you interpret from your dream about being in space with your childhood pet could serve as the inspiration for your next artwork.

Burn some incense
and sit quietly
enjoying the aroma.
Let your thoughts
stray to wherever
they want to go.

TURN YOUR FACE TO THE SUN AND THE SHADOWS FALL BEHIND YOU.

Maori proverb

Visit a museum dedicated to something you have no current interest in – you may be pleasantly surprised. It's easy to feel burnt out with an interest you are passionate about; you can explore every avenue excitedly, but feel as if you have hit a brick wall after a while in a search for something new.

A museum is a treasure trove of inspiration. For example, if you have visited an exhibit on feudal Japan, think about how a woman from that time may have looked; why not write about her, or even draw her? What about the objects she may have used in her everyday life? How could a historical woman influence a modern-day person?

Find an online community
for people in your profession.
Arrange or attend a social
networking event and
meet some new people.

LiE ON the GRaSS aND
WatCh the SKy.
See the PatteRNS
iN the CLOUDS.

Find yourself a 'positivity trigger'.
This can be anything which has good
connotations for you – a key-ring,
a photo, or even a small stone or
shell you can keep in your pocket,
and take out any time you need a
boost. Take a moment of time to
remember and appreciate all the good
experiences you have had, and with
that the sad ones too. Then focus
once more on the present time and
how you're feeling once again.

Learn to acknowledge all the lessons you have learned over time, then add those accomplishments and achievements to the memories you have with your 'positivity trigger'. Soon, every time you need a quick mood boost you will realise how small a sad moment is in comparison to all the good times. You will also learn the value of a sad moment, what makes it upsetting, and how you can find happiness once more.

DON'T JUDGE
EACH DAY BY
THE HARVEST
YOU REAP
BUT BY THE
SEEDS THAT
YOU PLANT.

Robert Louis Stevenson

Find out where the highest
natural point in your area is and
(as long as it's not dangerous!)
visit it to experience the view.

IF YOU HAVE BUILT
CASTLES IN THE AIR,
YOUR WORK NEED
NOT BE LOST; THAT
IS WHERE THEY
SHOULD BE. NOW
PUT FOUNDATIONS
UNDER THEM.

Henry David Thoreau

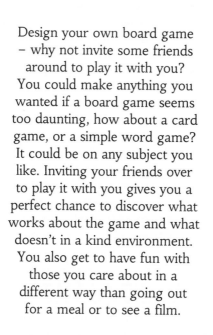

Design your own board game – why not invite some friends around to play it with you? You could make anything you wanted if a board game seems too daunting, how about a card game, or a simple word game? It could be on any subject you like. Inviting your friends over to play it with you gives you a perfect chance to discover what works about the game and what doesn't in a kind environment. You also get to have fun with those you care about in a different way than going out for a meal or to see a film.

Go to the insect house at your local zoo, or natural history museum, and watch the way that leafcutter ants work together to achieve their goal.

ONE IS
NOT BORN
a genius,
ONE BECOMES
a genius.

Simone de Beauvoir

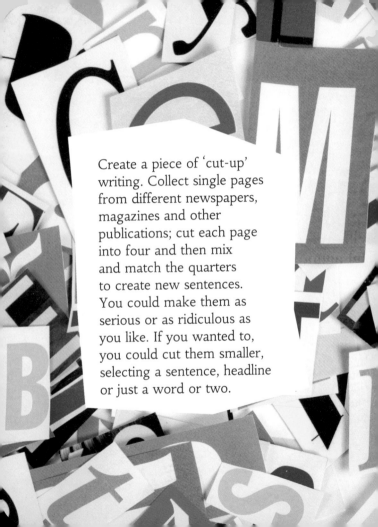

Create a piece of 'cut-up' writing. Collect single pages from different newspapers, magazines and other publications; cut each page into four and then mix and match the quarters to create new sentences. You could make them as serious or as ridiculous as you like. If you wanted to, you could cut them smaller, selecting a sentence, headline or just a word or two.

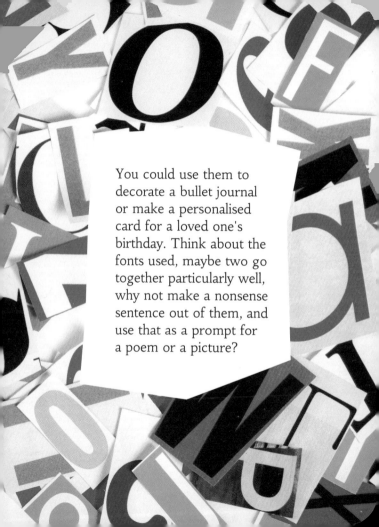

You could use them to decorate a bullet journal or make a personalised card for a loved one's birthday. Think about the fonts used, maybe two go together particularly well, why not make a nonsense sentence out of them, and use that as a prompt for a poem or a picture?

Try to write
a song using

only   notes.
            three

THE POWER OF IMAGINATION MAKES US INFINITE.

John Muir

Decorate your desk at work or at home with pictures of people or places that inspire you, calm you or motivate you. It's far too easy to fall into feeling stuck at work even if you are lucky enough to work from home. Keep positive pictures around to remind you of your goals. A picture of your family on a beautiful beach can remind you of the fun you shared but also serve as inspiration for the next holiday. If you work in a stressful environment, then a picture that can also serve as a 'happy place' can help keep you calm for when your surroundings take their toll.

Work your way through
the highest rated films of
all time – starting with
*The Shawshank
Redemption* and ending
up with the likes of
High School Musical...
you never know what
you might enjoy!

Speak few words,
but say them with quietude
and sincerity and they
will be long-lasting.

Lao Tzu

Go to the beach and dig your toes into the sand. Listen to the waves on the shore. Think about the colour of the sea, the taste of the salty air. Think of one word which perfectly sums up what your senses are experiencing.

Sleep outside
under the
open sky.

Make a fruit salad using no less than eight different fruits – try adding a dash of Grand Marnier to give it a bit of oomph! You might not want to add the brandy, but making a fruit salad can be a fantastic exercise in realising you might be eating bland, boring meals. Shaking it up a bit can add some excitement back into mealtimes. You could also use the opportunity to teach any children you know about food and get them involved in the creative process that is cooking. They may suggest adding ice cream, whipped cream, or even sprinkles to decorate; after all, why not?

Make your own ice lollies
using only natural ingredients

– or have a go at
ice cream if you're
feeling adventurous.

Try learning a
new language.
Download an app
or buy a 'teach
yourself' book, and
commit to learning
five new words or
phrases per day.

IF OPPORTUNITY DOESN'T KNOCK,

BUILD A DOOR.

Milton Berle

IT IS NEVER TOO LATE

TO BE WHAT YOU MIGHT HAVE BEEN.

George Eliot

*Poetry is the
one place where
people can speak
their original
human mind.*

Allen Ginsberg

Watch an outdoor performance – there are always classical concerts or Shakespeare performances during the summer.

Walk or cycle slowly down a road
and imagine who lives in each house.
Create a dramatic story for each one
– a secret addiction, a love affair or
some literal skeletons in closets!

Go boating...

MY HEART LEAPS UP WHEN I BEHOLD A RAINBOW IN THE SKY: SO WAS IT WHEN MY LIFE BEGAN, SO IS IT NOW I AM A MAN.

William Wordsworth

Find a piece of art, literature or music that is at least 2,000 years old, and create its modern counterpart. It can be hard to think of something that hasn't already been done before, so have a look at what has already been created and see if there is a fresh take on it. Think about all that you can tell has changed, for instance, the instruments used to create the music. Think of a way to

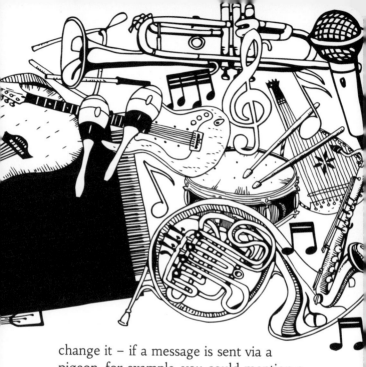

change it – if a message is sent via a pigeon, for example, you could mention a mobile phone. A pigeon and a mobile both make sounds; could you link the sounds somehow? Would you change everything or just a little to make it comedic? Could you create something new entirely?

IT IS IN VAIN TO
SAY THAT HUMAN
BEINGS OUGHT TO
BE SATISFIED WITH
TRANQUILLITY:

THEY MUST HAVE
ACTION; AND THEY
WILL MAKE IT IF THEY
CANNOT FIND IT.

Charlotte Brontë

Look outside and count how many different shades and colours you can see. Think of the perfect word to describe each tone: olive, pistachio, lawn green, jungle green, mint, chartreuse.

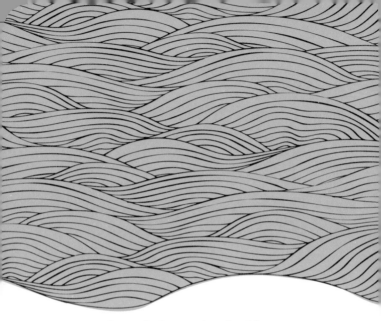

Try going through the weekend without checking the time – ignore your clock/watch/ phone and simply act on impulse. Try not to make plans with friends and family at a certain time – after all, you may end up naturally turning up far too late or not at all. Instead, focus on doing things you actually want to do. By not having alarms or your phone beeping to tell you of a new email from work, you can spend your

time doing things you actually enjoy. When was the last time you read a book uninterrupted, went for a walk along the seafront, or just spent time with a loved one without feeling as if you might need to leave any moment? Taking time to focus on yourself and the things you enjoy is healthy.

Go outside and photograph at least five different animals.

Get lost. Walk down an unexplored road or path and see where it leads.

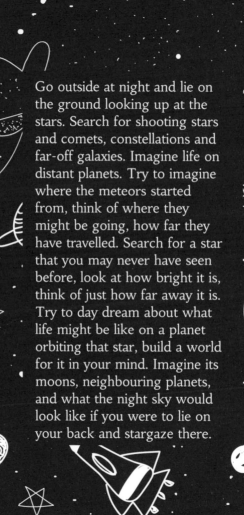

Go outside at night and lie on the ground looking up at the stars. Search for shooting stars and comets, constellations and far-off galaxies. Imagine life on distant planets. Try to imagine where the meteors started from, think of where they might be going, how far they have travelled. Search for a star that you may never have seen before, look at how bright it is, think of just how far away it is. Try to day dream about what life might be like on a planet orbiting that star, build a world for it in your mind. Imagine its moons, neighbouring planets, and what the night sky would look like if you were to lie on your back and stargaze there.

First say
to
yourself
what you
would
be;

AND THEN DO WHAT YOU HAVE TO DO.

Epictetus

Treat yourself to a long bubble
bath, complete with candles
and some relaxing music in the
background. Let your mind wander.

Plan out the screenplay
for the film of your
life so far. Work out
which actors will play
all the main parts.

A WISE MAN WILL MAKE MORE

OPPORTUNITIES

THAN HE FINDS.

Francis Bacon

Mindfulness Day: Close your eyes and breathe as slowly as possible. Become aware of all the things you can feel: the weight of your body on your chair, your hair against your forehead, a slight breeze through a window. Notice how you are sitting, how you have placed your hands on your lap or the armrest. Pay attention to how your body feels as you are sitting, noting any ache or pain you may have. Listen to all the sounds around you, taking note of each one. Make sure to focus on your breath – each time you find your mind wandering, remember to come back to your breath as a point of focus. Use your breath as an anchor to the present time, but also forgive yourself should your mind wander – mindfulness takes practice.

Enjoy the

little things,

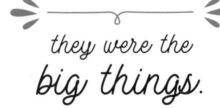

**FOR
ONE DAY
YOU MAY
LOOK BACK
AND REALISE**

they were the

big things.

Robert Brault

Make seasonal decorations and use them to decorate your garden or the front of your home – or to give away as presents!

Use aural stimuli to help you relax. Try
listening to sound effects such as softly
lapping waves or birds twittering (you can
find them online) to blot out other noises.
If you have chosen to listen to the sound
of a fireplace take a moment with your
eyes closed to imagine what that fireplace
looks like. Is it a hot fire, surrounded by
friends and family, or is it just the last
embers of a once flaming pyre. Spend
some time just listening to the sounds
you have chosen, even if it is simply the
sounds around you of office chatter, calm
your breathing and allow the sounds
to take you somewhere different.

THE MORE YOU LOSE YOURSELF IN SOMETHING BIGGER THAN YOURSELF, THE MORE ENERGY YOU WILL HAVE.

Norman Vincent Peale

Volunteer to help tend the grounds at your local park or communal garden. Just getting outside doing things works wonders for you. See if your local places need any sort of help, and offer your services, especially if you feel you have no valuable skill to offer. You may simply do nothing more than pick up rubbish, but that is a big part in making sure communal spaces stay looking beautiful and more importantly, safe for use. Helping out around where you live creates a better understanding of your local area, who you live with, and the troubles surrounding it. After all, you may like looking after your own garden, but few people get to truly appreciate all the care you pour into it, whereas in a public, communal space, everyone will.

AN OPEN HEART IS
AN OPEN MIND.

Dalai Lama

...SOONER OR LATER,
THE MAN WHO
WINS
IS THE MAN WHO
THINKS
HE CAN.

Walter D. Wintle

Design your own typeface
(drawn out by hand or using a computer),
or choose an unusual one.
Use it to write an inspirational message.

Read a book set in a country you've never visited. Travelling to other countries for inspiration can be expensive, and whilst it is good to visit different places, learning about other cultures and religions, it's not always so easy to drop everything and tour New Zealand for a month. A book is one of the best ways of gaining new inspiration without having to travel, but also a way to avoid suffering culture shock if you do eventually visit. Japan may sound like a dream holiday, but it has a completely different language, religion and culinary options to sample. Reading about a person living in that country can let you know a little about what to expect when the plane touches down, so you're not left so bewildered and clutching a travel guide in desperation.

Take a duvet day or unscheduled holiday and spend the day doing absolutely nothing at all! After all, you deserve it, and it's important to remember that if you work hard, you get to play hard too. Spending a day doing absolutely nothing but reading a book or catching up on a favourite box set is just as important as the time you spend working. Don't forget to prioritise yourself by recharging your batteries. Even if your idea of a day doing nothing means reorganising your home, training for a marathon and cooking a feast for your entire family, it's still vital time spent doing nothing but looking after yourself. The next day, you will find yourself refreshed and much more willing to spend time on those tasks you don't really want to do, but have to.

Embrace silence, whether you are alone or in the company of others. It is healthy to take a step back from the noise and embrace the situation you are in, whether this involves drinking your morning coffee outside instead of in front of the television, or letting silence between friends remain silent instead of filling it with artificial conversation.

Buy a small-sized,
plain paper notebook
and create a flip-page
animation of something
that makes
you smile.

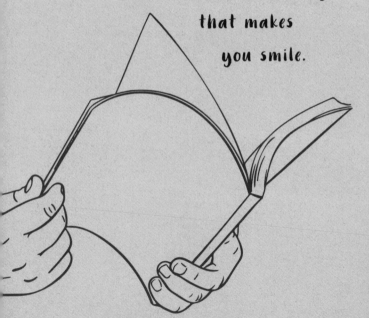

THE PESSIMIST SEES
DIFFICULTY IN
EVERY OPPORTUNITY.

THE OPTIMIST SEES
THE OPPORTUNITY IN
EVERY DIFFICULTY.

Winston Churchill

Far away there in the
sunshine are my highest
aspirations. I may not
reach them, but I can look
up and see their beauty,
believe in them, and try to
follow where they lead.

Louisa May Alcott

Put on your favourite song and sing at the top of your voice. Fill your lungs with air and release the build-up of tension and stress.

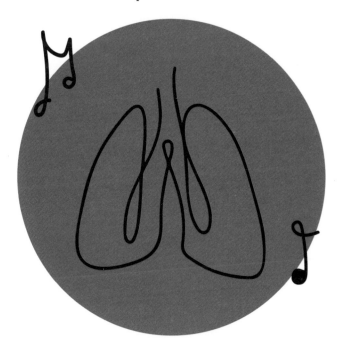

Revisit the neighbourhood in which you grew up. Take an hour or two to wander around and soak up the memories. A trip down memory lane can help you appreciate what you have at the moment, how far you've come, and to also note any childhood friends you may still have. It is also a good opportunity to forgive yourself for any childhood mishaps you

haven't yet been able to come to terms with. Taking time to appreciate where you have come from and to remember those you grew up with can lead to being at peace with yourself. You can even find some inspiration in reliving those childhood journeys that made you the person you are today, after all, what might have happened if you had chosen to do something differently?

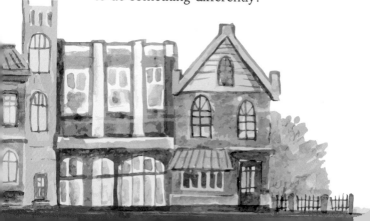

Fill one side of A4 paper with your argument for something you feel passionately about.

Fill the other side with the strongest counter-argument you can think of.

TRY TO GO AN ENTIRE
DAY WITHOUT SAYING
ANYTHING NEGATIVE.

YOU CAN'T USE UP
CREATIVITY.
THE MORE YOU USE,
THE MORE YOU HAVE.

Maya Angelou

Light a candle and focus on
the movement of the flame
and the quality of the light.
Allow yourself to just be
still and quiet, for as long as
you like. Enjoy the silence.

It's not where you take things from, it's where you take them to.

Jean-Luc Godard

IMAGE CREDITS

Every reasonable effort has been made by
the publisher to trace and acknowledge
the copyright holders of material used
in this book. If any errors or omissions
are brought to light, the publisher will
endeavour to rectify them in any reprints
or future editions.

If you're interested in finding out more about our books, find us on Facebook at **Summersdale Publishers** and follow us on Twitter at **@Summersdale**.

www.summersdale.com